Designing a Life:
From House to Haven

By Sarah Symonds

Editor: Janelle Franz
Cover Photo: Philipp Berndt
Cover Design: Sarah Symonds

About the Author

Sarah Symonds is a popular lifestyle blogger at www.graceinmyspace.com who focuses on teaching her readers to live and design in grace. She has been featured digitally by Better Homes and Gardens and American Farmhouse Style Magazine, and is a Featured Blogger and Style Icon with Joss & Main.

Sarah has a Master's degree in Business Management and is a self-taught entrepreneur and stylist who focuses on DIY, home design, and being a haven-maker. In her writing you will find elements of faith and values woven into the fabric of what she teaches. Sarah resides in Michigan with her husband and two beautiful children.

For daily inspiration and ideas, visit www.graceinmyspace.com and join me on my own journey of creating a haven. Sign up for my weekly newsletter at www.graceinmyspace.com/free-printables.

Copyright

Table of Contents

1. Adjust your Mindset: Design a Life to Create Your Haven......................................7
   Haven Mission Statement
2. The Basics: Pre-Design Stage......................12
   Define Your Needs
   Evaluate the Problem(s)
   Set Realistic Expectations
3. Establish a Vision + Set Goals......................16
   Create a Design Vision
   Define Inspirational Design Elements
   Be Realistic in Design
   Set Short Term & Long Term Goals
   Edit Existing Decor
4. Design Process: Let's Break It Down...............22
5. Implementation..24
   Implement Design Plan
6. Design Quick Tips......................................25
7. Real Life Problems, Solved...........................27
8. You're a Haven Maker.................................34
9. Workbook...36

Designing a Life: From House to Haven

Welcome and thank you for taking the next step in designing a life you love with *Designing a Life: From House to Haven*!

This book is intended to give you simple steps to design a life inside your home.

My goal is to help you create a life-giving haven. A place to belong. A place of comfort and peace. A place where you can rest and be rejuvenated. A place to live life with ease.

A well-decorated house is not the ultimate goal. The real goal? Creating a haven and changing your mindset towards design.

Decor and design shouldn't be stagnant or impersonal. Rather, it should flow with personality, evolve with your tastes, and be a representation of pieces that make your heart sing.

Fill a house with decor and it remains just a house. Design a life-giving space and it becomes a haven.

It's time to start creating your haven and join the community of haven makers! Whether you want to tackle an entire home renovation or simply update one space, this book will guide you through the process.

Make sure to use your workbook to jot down ideas as you read and let's get started!

~ Sarah Symonds
www.graceinmyspace.com

Download Your Workbook

Before you dive into this book, look over the workbook starting on page 36.

Then, go to my website to download your free 10 step printable workbook if you need extra copies! Utilize this workbook for each step in the design phase and print a new copy with each new project you plan to tackle.

Download Your Free Workbook at www.graceinmyspace.com/designing-a-life-from-house-to-haven-workbook.

1. Adjust Your Mindset: Design a Life to Create Your Haven

ha·ven
hāvən/: a place of safety or refuge.
home
hōm/: the place where one lives permanently

Consider these two definitions. Where would you rather reside? In a permanent place or in a refuge?

Your house is intended to be more than just a home. A healthy home is a space of safety and refuge. A haven. Creating a haven goes so far beyond making a space pretty and it begins with your mindset.

You'll see throughout this book that your mindset towards design is imperative to creating a haven. So let's talk about how to align your mindset towards your home as the first step before we dive into design.

Workbook Step 1: Use your workbook to walk through the steps of knowing yourself and creating a haven mission statement.

First, Know Yourself

You cannot create a haven without knowing yourself. Be a student of yourself and the people who occupy your home prior to any design decisions. Be intentional in thinking through some of the following questions. Take your time to really get to know yourself in the process.

See Workbook Step 1 for a place to jot down notes:

What makes you tense? What makes you relax? What are your time limitations? Do you need a cozy corner carved out for you to recharge or would you rather spend all your time in a family room surrounded by others?

Are you single? Do you have a roommate to consider? Are you married? Team up with your spouse if he/she cares to have input in design decisions. Do you have kids? Pets? Remember that they will live here too!

Design is insignificant if the choices you make are "on trend" but create *tension* in your home.

Real Life Example: I have white walls. I LOVE the beautiful way they bring a calming atmosphere to our space and make my decor pop. However, I also have two kids with dirty hands and feet and a large dog who sprays mud everywhere when she shakes dry.

Guess what I don't *always* love? White walls. My white walls are a good design, but in reality they can cause angst because of the little things that go into maintaining them.

The moral of the story is: Know yourself and your family and make design decisions based on the kind of life you plan to live in your home.

Create Your Haven Mission Statement

Now that you have intentionally considered your personality and the personalities of those who occupy your home, let's create a haven mission statement.

What is a haven mission statement and why should you create one? A mission statement is simply an organized way of communicating your values and overall goals. Companies create them to give purpose and direction to their entire entity. Individuals and families should create one for the same purpose and to help define the mindset you will adopt as you dive into design.

State your values and goals for your home in order to cut out the noise that we are often barraged with. Design trends, celebrity recommendations, the latest fad: none of these matter if they don't align with your own personal values and goals.

Define Haven

Take a moment and define haven in your own words in your workbook.

Here are some words that come to mind for me. Safe. Comfortable. Relaxed. Warm. Happy family. Rest. Retreat. Cozy. Inviting. Refreshing. God honoring.

Different personality types will think of different words. Perhaps some of these came to mind for you. Bright. Exciting. Energizing. Creative. Nature. Amenities. Bold. Large. Small.

Whatever your personality, it is important to remember that as you design your home you are designing it to be a haven. A retreat where you can rest and be restored alongside your family.

Once you've defined what a haven is to you, move on to considering the desired atmosphere of your haven.

Desired Atmosphere

Next, throw traditional design ideas out the window and decide the type of **atmosphere** you need your haven to have. What atmosphere do you need to create, through design, to consider your home a haven? Here are some questions to consider:

- Does it need to be organized or can you live with clutter?
- Do you want it to be a landing place for friends and family or are you more private?
- Do you want to feel energized or restful in your space?
- Do you thrive on bright spaces or do you prefer moodier lighting?

Life Goals

Next, determine what you want to accomplish in your home. Think through how you use your home to accomplish those goals and jot those down in your workbook. Here are some additional questions to spur your brainstorming session.

- Do you need to designate space to work from home or provide a home school?
- Do you want to provide a safe space for young children to play?
- Do you need a separate space for a business?
- Will you be home the majority of the day or do you spend your time elsewhere?
- How big is your family and what need do you have for growth or downsizing?
- Is meal prep a large part of your life or do you enjoy take out?

Your definition of haven, coupled with your desired atmosphere, and the life goals you want to achieve, all give you a jumping off point to create a mission statement for your haven.

Haven Definition + Desired Atmosphere + Life Goals = Haven Mission Statement

Real Life Example:

My personal haven mission statement:

To create a safe, welcoming, cozy and organized environment for my family to live, thrive and learn in while designating both family and individual spaces each person can relax and recharge in. To be a steward of the haven God provides for us while being a reflection of God's goodness to all who enter in person or via Grace In My Space. To enjoy my haven as a reflection of my own creativity and our family's personality.

Your mission statement will be different from mine, and that is ok! You are creating YOUR haven, not mine or anyone else's. Take a moment to create a haven mission statement in the last section of Step 1 in your workbook.

Once you have conquered the idea that you are designing a life, rather than a home, it is natural to transform your house into a haven.

With that mindset, let's talk about some practical steps to get started.

2. The Basics: Pre-Design Stage

Before we discuss design, we must examine the purpose of your home. Good design is highly valuable, but if it doesn't serve a purpose or meet one of your goals then it can hinder the overall goal of creating a haven. Let's break this down.

Workbook Step 2: Consider the following information and write out your family needs, keeping your haven mission statement in mind.

First Steps

Define Your Needs

Now that you have thought through the personality traits of yourself and your family, take a moment to consider what your haven needs to provide to you. This can be as specific as "I need four bedrooms, two bathrooms and three washing machines because I have four kids in sports" or as general as "I need non-white walls so I'm not burdened by the upkeep."

Jot these down in Step 2 of your workbook.

This will help lay the groundwork for creating a haven with the proper mindset. And don't worry, we will get into some more design specific tips in chapter four and solve some real-life problems in chapter five.

Define Your Design Style….Or Don't

Now that you have the proper mindset, a haven mission statement, and a list of needs to accomplish that mission, let's start talking about design!

Do you want to know the surprisingly simple way to define your design style? Don't.

Does that seem counterintuitive? Everyone should define their style prior to starting a project, shouldn't they? Wrong!

Let's take design icon, Joanna Gaines, for example. How would you define her design style? Farmhouse. Modern. Contemporary. Traditional. Industrial. Chances are, you've seen all of those design styles in her work. That is because *design is meant to be fluid.*

Design trends will come and go. Some even come, go, and then come back again! And that is OK! Don't limit yourself by determining that you need to stay within the design trend of X style.

The goal is not to design a space that will remain stagnant for the rest of your life. The goal is to design a haven that is reminiscent of your life and meets your needs.

And if there is one thing that is guaranteed in life, it is change. Design shouldn't be any different. Change is good. Change is interesting. Change is inevitable. Change is fun!

So don't stress over how to define your design style. Chances are, it will be different in a year or two. We will work on what you should do instead in the next chapter.

Evaluate the Problem

Now that you've established a haven mission statement and defined your needs to create that haven, it is time to evaluate the problem. Analyze your home. What specific elements are standing in the way of creating a haven?

Workbook Step 3: Utilize your workbook as you work through this section.

Is your dining room table too small to accommodate your family? Do you feel like the atmosphere isn't in line with your desires? Is the color scheme no longer to your taste? Does the blueprint prevent you from accomplishing a life goal? Whatever it is, be specific and exacting.

Real Life Example

Often the things that you think you dislike are misunderstood. For instance, one design project I worked on had a bulky brown brick fireplace in a small room. My initial response was to tear it out and replace it with something more to scale. However, after examining the room more closely, I realized it was not the size of the fireplace that bothered me, but the dark color of the bricks. It made the space feel small and dingy.

My solution was to whitewash the brick! Instantly the space was brighter and the smaller appearing fireplace became a beautiful focal point of the room. Taking the time to evaluate the real problem saved countless hours of work and tons of money!

After evaluating the true problem(s), interpret what kind of solution you think may fix the issue. At this point in the process, you are just speculating to get a better idea of how involved the project may be. Narrow it down to one of these four categories.

To fix the problem, do you need to:

1. *Rearrange.* Simply move decor around, change furniture layouts, put an organizing system in place, or change the function of a room.
2. *Refresh.* Add new decor, buy furniture, or change color schemes.
3. *Remodel.* Update paint colors, replace outdated fixtures or finishes, or buy bigger ticket items like new appliances, windows or doors.
4. *Renovate.* Restore flooring, take down walls, replace cabinets, move plumbing and electrical, add room additions, or otherwise change the structure of a home.

Set Realistic Expectations

My absolute number one tip for designing a haven is to be *realistic*. Unrealistic expectations are a sure-fire way to become discouraged and frustrated when seeking to make your house into a haven.

Workbook Step 4: Use the space provided to define realistic expectations for each project you wish to tackle.

Be realistic about:
- Budget
  - Establish a realistic budget prior to planning decor, design, or renovations. Make sure your significant other is on board! Even small pieces of decor can get pricey quickly so do your research ahead of time.
- Renovation limitations
  - Do you want to take out a wall or change the layout of a kitchen? Make sure you do your homework first. Is the wall load bearing? Can you move plumbing and still stay in budget? Almost anything is possible in the construction world but you have to have the budget and expertise to make it happen.
- Timeframes
  - Plan for your plans to go awry. Setting realistic timeframes for everything from simple decorating, painting projects, or full-on renovations is important for your overall sanity. Whether you are working with a contractor, designer, or doing it DIY style, make sure you discuss timeframes in depth.
- Your own ability
  - Are you an avid DIYer? Or does it scare you to think about painting a room? Know your own limitations and abilities prior to tackling a project! Just about anyone can paint a room but not everyone is comfortable with it. If you know you'll need help, there is no harm in asking a talented friend or even hiring a designer or contractor to work with for larger projects.

3. Establish a Design Vision + Set Goals

You've come so far! You've done the hard work of creating your haven mission statement to help align your mindset towards design. You've defined your needs, established the problems you want to fix, and set realistic expectations. Now it's time to design.

Whether you are designing one room or an entire house, take the time to think big picture and create a design vision. Next, set short term and long term goals for yourself. This will help you accomplish your final goal of implementing your design vision within the parameters of your haven mission statement.

Let's walk through some basic Q+A's to help you establish a design vision and set goals.

Workbook Steps 5 & 6: Take notes in your workbook to help you establish a design vision.

Basic Question: How Do I Create A Design Vision?
Answer: First, Create Inspiration/Vision Boards on Pinterest

Define what makes your heart sing with vision boards. One way to do this is to study other people's designs first to see what sticks out to you.

Do you remember the days of ripping out pages of magazines with spaces that inspire you? Do you still do that? Step it up a notch and use Pinterest where there are thousands of inspirational photos of design and decor. You can follow me on Pinterest at www.pinterest.com/ graceinmyspace.

Remember, there is a difference between design that you enjoy and design that inspires. I *enjoy* many styles but not all of them *inspire* me.

Example: I love minimalistic design styles. It is refreshing to me. However, when I try to implement it into my own home it just feels unfinished and sparse. So while I enjoy it, it doesn't inspire me.

On the other hand, if I'm in a space with a beautifully arranged collection, lots of layers, or beautiful textures it makes me stop and stare. Because I am inspired!

That's why you must do your homework and define what inspires you before diving into any design project.

Pinterest Strategy: Steps 5 & 6 of Your Workbook

As you browse Pinterest, create a separate board for each project. When you see a photo you are inspired by, pin it to the appropriate board.

If you see an image and your first reaction is to toss it to the side, then the style it embodies does NOT belong in your home. It could be something Joanna Gaines designed herself but if it doesn't resonate with you then don't try to copy it just because it is popular.

Limit your design plans to examples that fully inspire you. Give it the "stop and stare" test. If you don't stop and stare, then it most likely doesn't strike you with inspiration.
Create a separate Pinterest board for each room that you want to work on and start pinning spaces that make your heart sing. Don't forget the "stop and stare" test. If you don't love it, then don't pin it. Cluttering up your boards with spaces that you simply enjoy (but don't make your heart sing) will only confuse you later on in the process.

If that means each Pinterest board only has 10 pictures, that is ok! You've just made it easier to define the elements that inspire you.

Once you find inspirational examples, define what you love about them in step 6 of your workbook. Is it the way a centerpiece is arranged on a table? Is it the color palette of a room? Is it the use of texture? Is it clean lines and sleek design? Write it down in your workbook!

No detail is too small to help you see how multiple design styles can be interwoven to suit your tastes, and in turn, to help you create your design vision. These detailed assessments will give you the foundation to creating your own design plans. They will be the reference point that you can go back to when deciding how you want to design your space.

Workbook Step 7

Basic Question: Once I have my vision boards, what's my next step?
Answer: The next step is to be realistic with the space you have.

Kitchens and bathrooms are often the hardest rooms to design because layout is such a huge element. If your heart sings over kitchens with a center island but you don't have space for such luxury, then your vision needs to include a realistic alternative.

If every interior inspiration photo has an all white color palette, then make sure you evaluate if it is practical for your lifestyle. Do you have young kids or pets that will leave smudges all over your walls and cause you anxiety? Then white might not be the best option. Go for a slightly darker alternative to mask those kinds of issues.

Remember, keep the mindset that you are creating a *life* and a *haven*. If your design choices conflict with your lifestyle then you're not creating a haven. You're creating a long-term trial.

Complete Step 7 of your workbook with this in mind.

On the flip side, does that mean you can't have a nice home because you're living life? Of course not.

The number one question I get from readers is, "How do you display decor with small children? Don't they break things all the time?"

Yes. Things get broken. Does that mean I plan to design my house like a plastic bubble until they are grown? No!

My solution: Keep my haven mission statement in mind and *train them*. Raise them with a decorated home and they will learn how to behave in one. Teach them what is ok to touch and what is not. Teach them where they are allowed to kick a ball and where they aren't. And go back to chapter one and remember that your mindset is of utmost importance in this type of situation especially.

See chapter 6, *Real Life Problems, Solved*, for more suggestions on designing with a family in mind.

Workbook Step 8

Basic Question: I have my vision, I know what's realistic, and I'm still at a standstill.
Answer: Set Your Short Term and Long Term Goals

Often the hardest part to designing a haven is knowing where to start. Simplify the process by creating short term and long term goals for each project in Step 8 of your workbook. Remember to keep in mind your haven mission statement, budget, limitations and timeframes. Everything you've analyzed up to this point works together to move your design forward.

Real Life Example:

Project: Living Room Refresh
You want to update:
- Paint
- Wall Decor & Accents
- Layout

    Short Term Goal: Research which accents can be changed within the established budget. (Only have $300 for the budget? Then you most likely won't be able to include larger pieces like a new rug. But you can certainly afford new paint and a few new accents!)

    Short Term Goal: Paint the room!
Paint is one of the most transformative, fast, affordable, and easy ways to update a space. It can usually be completed in one weekend depending on the size of the room.

    Long Term Goal: Shop for and find new decor and accents that fit your budget and vision. Why is this a long term goal? Because sometimes finding just the right piece takes time!!

    You can design a house from one home department store in one day. But designing a haven takes long-term vision and time.

    Don't rush design. The most interesting homes are the ones that are collected over time. Each piece tells a story or serves a purpose and is connected to the life of the home owner.

    Enjoy the process. Don't stress over completion. Achieve your goals one at a time and be patient with yourself and the design process.

    Take some time to really consider your goals. Use Step 8 in your workbook to solidify them.

Workbook Step 9

Basic Question: I've set my goals, but I feel overwhelmed by my existing decor. How do I incorporate what I have into my design plans?
Answer: Edit your home.

One of the biggest mistakes you can make in creating your haven is to try to force existing decor you no longer love into your design. Realistically, perhaps you *will* have to live with your outdated couch until it fits into your plans and budget to purchase a new one. However, for smaller decor items and pieces that may be unnecessary (ex: those five end tables you've stored for 10 years but never used) you should edit!

How do you edit? Walk through your home with your haven mission statement, design vision, and goals in mind. Consider your existing decor and furniture and decide whether or not you love it and can incorporate it into your plans. If you don't love it, can't repurpose it, or it doesn't serve a purpose, then edit it. You can sell it and use those funds to increase your budget or you can donate it.

Outdated decor and design will not serve a purpose in creating your haven. Remember that design is fluid and your tastes will evolve with time, so change is ok! Change is a stepping stone to the life-long goal of creating your haven.

Step 9 of your workbook gives you a place to break down how you view your existing possessions. Use this space to flush out how you will either edit, incorporate or repurpose these pieces into your design plans.

4. Design Process: Let's Break It Down

Now that you have a good grasp on the forethought and planning that goes into designing a haven, let's talk design. My goal in this book is to encourage you to think of designing your home as a life-long process. You aren't simply decorating or renovating. You are creating a space where you and your family can thrive. A **haven**.

With that in mind, let's simplify each step we've talked about so far. Here is the basic design process broken down into 10 steps:

1. State your Haven Mission Statement
2. Define Your Needs
3. Evaluate the Problem(s) (What do you want to change?)
   - Set Your Budget
   - Determine your limitations
   - Establish a realistic timeline
4. Set Realistic Expectations
5. Build Your Design Vision with your Haven Mission Statement in mind
6. Define Design Elements that Inspire You
7. Be Realistic with Design
8. Create Short Term and Long Term Goals
9. Edit Your Home
10. Implement (Up Next)
- Enjoy

You will notice that there are at least 9 steps to walk through prior to actually implementing your design plans. The forethought and planning stages of design are perhaps the most important. Without truly considering these steps in the design process, it will be difficult to create a haven.

For years I swung from one decor trend to another based on what was popular. I wasted a lot of money. I accumulated a lot of stuff I didn't love. I repainted a lot of rooms. I had a lot of yard sales. And it was all because I never considered my home design to be a part of the haven I was creating for my family.

Walking through these 9 steps prior to implementing design will help you save time, money, energy and, hopefully, a little bit of your sanity.

Rushed design can result in disappointment if it is implemented without consideration for how it aligns with your haven mission statement. Don't skip these first 9 steps and assume that designing your haven can be accomplished in one weekend. Being thoughtful of your design plans prior to implementation will help you accomplish your ultimate goals.

5. Implementation

Whew! We've covered a lot of ground. You've done so much work to get to this stage of the process. It may seem like a daunting task to break down each future project in this way, but my hope is that you come to enjoy the *process* as much as the final product as you design your haven.

You've done all the leg work, you've laid the foundation, and you've set your goals. Now it's time to implement. Use your responses to steps 1-9 in your workbook to guide the implementation of your design plans. Your short term and long term goals should clearly communicate the steps you need to take to move forward.

Use **Step 10 of your workbook** to concisely summarize your design plan and then go for it!

6. Design Quick Tips

Keeping the previous chapters in mind, let's move on to discuss simple ideas you can incorporate into you design plans to add interest. These are not intended to be "must do" items to tack on to your list. Rather, they are intended to be a part of your brainstorming process to help spur your creativity.

As you read each suggestion, consider whether or not it aligns with your haven mission statement and ultimate design vision. If it doesn't, scratch it off the list! If it does, add it to your short or long term goals to see if it is feasible for your design situation.

Design Quick Tip Suggestions

- Use paint to transform a space overnight. If a room is feeling bland, outdated, dingy or dark, try changing the wall color before you spend money on new furniture or decor.
- Use color unexpectedly: Think painted ceilings, accent walls, painted furniture, rugs, or artwork to spruce up a space visually.
- Add layers for interest. Here are some basic examples of how to accomplish this:
    1. Rather than hang one large piece of art over a fireplace, layer three pieces of varying size directly on the mantel.
    2. Layer a more interesting rug on top of a larger basic natural fiber rug to add warmth and interest.
    3. Stack similar items (such as platters, collections or everyday items like plates and bowls) on open shelving.
    4. Layer wreaths or artwork overtop of other wall decor.
- Group unrelated objects on a gallery wall for more character.
- Conversely, group large impact identical frames in a grid for a gallery wall. Frame what you love! This could be

family photos, artwork, or a combination as long as the frames are cohesive.

- Display similar items as a collection. Grouping them has more impact than if they are scattered around your home. (Ex: bottles, pitchers, collectibles, bowls, ironstone, or even artwork)
- Create zones in an open concept home by using rugs or furniture to define boundaries.
- Think outside the box. Do you love the pattern of a small rug but don't think it's practical for your family? Hang it on a wall. Do you have an old workbench that no longer serves its original purpose? Turn it into a desk or dining table. Have your children outgrown the need for a playroom? Transform it into a personal retreat, office, or guest room.
- Use baskets, trays or boxes to corral clutter or small objects. Even a stack of mail, your car keys and sunglasses will look more classy if they are grouped in a designated container.
- Go vertical. If you're short on space, take advantage of tall shelving or the tops of cupboards or furniture to display decor.

BONUS MATERIAL
7. Real Life Problems Solved

As you design your haven, you may run into one or more of these common problems. Just remember, designing a haven is not the same as designing a house.

It will take time and it is a process that you will have to learn and adjust to as your mindset towards design changes. In the meantime, here are some helpful solutions to common problems.

How do I accomplish my large design vision with a small budget?

No matter your budget, you can still make changes that will move you in the direction of creating a haven. Perhaps your design plan needs to include several stages over a longer time period in order to accomplish your goals. That is perfectly normal! Be patient with the process. However, here are some ideas for smaller budgets as you think through your goals.

- Under $100
    - Shop your home. Move existing decor from one room to another for a fresh feel.
    - Make a big impact with fresh paint (walls, cabinets, wood furniture).
    - Create a gallery of thrift store finds or free printables in affordable frames.
    - Add live plants to freshen a space.
    - Refinish existing furniture.
    - Do a decor swap with a similarly styled friend.
    - Reorganize existing furniture for a more family-friendly layout or to improve flow.
    - Simply organize! It is amazing how easily a house can be transformed if you establish a "home" for everyday items and keep it picked up and tidy.
- Under $500
  Implement any of the above, plus:
    - Refresh a room with new pillows, blankets or artwork.

- Add a defining piece of furniture such as a shelf, console table, rug or accent chair. Just ensure that it serves a purpose to move you towards your goals.
- Add new lighting to update a space.
- DIY kitchens or bathrooms by painting cabinetry or installing open shelving.

How do I incorporate sentimental heirlooms into my home when they may not suit my tastes?

This can be a tough situation for sentimental personalities. Take a step back from your attachment to the item and determine how it fits into your goals of creating a haven. If it is something you don't love but simply can't let go of, then try to repurpose it.

Can an old end table be repurposed into a plant stand? Can grandma's wardrobe become your TV cabinet? Can some items be passed on to other family members who may appreciate them more aesthetically?

At some point you may just need to consider whether or not storing something you don't love is a better choice than selling or gifting it to someone who will fully enjoy it.

How to do I create a color palette?

Head back to chapter 3. Remember your Pinterest vision boards? What are the common colors you are drawn to in other's homes? Start there.

Perhaps green keeps popping up in all your vision boards. Determine whether or not you want green to be your wall color for a big statement or if you'd rather subdue it as a main accent color.

From there, choose 2-3 coordinating colors and stick with that color palette for the majority of your home. This will make it feel cohesive and fluid.

For more assistance, I highly recommend searching for "whole house color palettes" on Pinterest! There are many beautiful options already designed and you can create a vision board specifically for this purpose.

Just be sure to test paint samples in your own home prior to purchasing large quantities. A paint color **will** look different on your walls than it does on your computer screen or in a magazine.

What is the proper rug size?

I'd like to say that this is a matter of preference, but this is one design rule that I really like to stick to. Too small of a rug can easily ruin the design around it while too large of a rug can look sloppy.

For a living room, your rug should be large enough that at least the front two legs of your couch and chairs can fit onto it. If you have a 12x20ft room and place a 4x6ft rug in the middle it will look out of place and unnecessary. Conversely, if you use an 12x15ft rug then you may as well just carpet the whole space.

Think of rugs as "zone keepers". If you want to create a living room zone, then buy a rug large enough for your furniture to rest on comfortably. If you're creating a dining room zone, then your dining room chairs should be able to be pulled back and still remain on the rug. If you want to zone an entryway, a 5x7 rug is usually a sufficient space to allow guests to come in and remove shoes without stepping off the rug.

Try to keep your rugs in scale with the size of the zone you are defining.

How can I "get the look" from design icons without it turning out like a Pinterest fail?

It happens to the best of us. Most of the time, it's because we didn't walk through the entire design process! What works for someone else's home will not work for yours if it isn't in line with your haven mission statement and design vision.

Rather than trying to copy other's examples, define what you love about the spaces they have designed. Perhaps you tried to recreate the boho look with dozens of plants when the real design element you loved was the use of pops of color. Or maybe you oversimplified your decor to achieve the minimalistic design style when you really just love the clean lines of the furniture in Scandinavian design.

This is why it is important to walk through the process and truly define the elements that are speaking to you prior to moving forward.

Also, remember from chapter 2 that it's important to know your own limitations. If you tried to build a dining room table but carpentry isn't your gift, then it is inevitable that you will become frustrated and discouraged. It is ok to hire a pro when you need to!

Otherwise, take the time to re-evaluate your design goals. Perhaps a short term goal should be moved to a long term goal to allow you the time, budget, and skill to accomplish it.

How do I brighten a room with little natural light?
Lighting is one of the most important, and often overlooked, elements of design. It can affect your mood, the way paint colors appear, and the functionality of a space. This is an awesome element to thoughtfully incorporate into your design.

Start with the large elements in your home. Light walls or floors will reflect more natural light whereas dark walls or floors absorb it. Then look at your furniture. Is everything dark? Consider painting dark bookcases or cabinets to lighten the space.

Next, add lighting. If a lack of natural light is the problem then the only way to combat that is to bring in artificial, unless you have the budget to add a window or door. If you have a larger budget then you can also consider adding hardwired canned lights or pendants, if appropriate. Otherwise, add floor lamps and a couple of table lamps along with your overhead lighting.

Look for LED bulbs that boast full-spectrum color to best mimic natural light.

How do I keep a space I've designed looking nice in the midst of children and pets and all things "life"?

In chapter 1 we discussed the mindset behind creating a haven. This is such an important concept to remember when considering designing with a family in mind. Often we are looking for a "trick" or "quick fix" to keeping a designed space looking pristine.

While there are many organizational strategies and pieces of furniture you can buy to corral clutter, it simply takes training your family to treat the space appropriately, as well as a lot of hard work, to clean and organize on a daily basis.

As you think through your personality and your needs, consider laying out ground rules for your family. Your rules will look different than mine, but could be something along the lines of:
1. Children must pick up toys/mess every night before screen/bed time.
2. Each family member is assigned one chore daily.
3. Rather than placing dirty dishes on the counter, family members must load them directly into the dishwasher.

These guidelines can be very simple and age appropriate, but are impactful in raising a family with the mindset that everyone has a responsibility towards the greater family unit and can help in creating a haven.

Children (and adults) have to be taught, will make mistakes, and will eventually learn from them.

Until then, you must remember that the haven you're creating for yourself and your family is more important than the **things** within it.

Don't let everyday messes make you feel as thought you've ruined your design. You've created a haven and that includes actually living in it!

How do I decorate large blank walls?
Expansive spaces are often a stumbling block in design. Too much on the walls and they look cluttered. Too little and they look out of proportion. So rather than designing the walls first, place your large pieces of furniture in a room and use those as anchor points for wall decor.

You can decorate above and around furniture with large scale art for those with simple tastes. If you like more layers and added interest then you can create tiered shelving with favorite mementos or use gallery walls (groupings of smaller objects) to display favorite decor.

The easiest and simplest approach: If you are working with a large wall then use large scale decor. The bigger the better (to an extent) to fill a space without over cluttering.

How do I incorporate my TV into decor?
Here are some quick fixes for incorporating the TV into your decor.
- Use it as the focal point for a simple gallery wall. Family photos would be a beautiful way to surround your TV. Depending on it's size, you can add a rectangle or square frame with large mats on either side of the TV as well as three above it. This encases your TV with precious memories! Just make sure the frames are substantial and identical for the most seamless design.

- Place open shelving or media furniture on either side of it! Use the shelves to display simple decor or books.
- Hide it! Nowadays there are many ways to cover up TVs with sliding barn doors, mirrors, framing or by placing it into a cupboard that has doors.
- Embrace it! It is becoming less and less common to find homes without a TV. If it's a daily part of your lifestyle, then decorate around it using some of the tactics above and enjoy it with your family.

What do I do when space is an issue?

Often people find space to be an issue when they've failed to accomplish the "editing" stage of design. If you're home is small, consider what is necessary to keep in order to accomplish your haven mission statement.

Perhaps one blanket per person is sufficient over 15 blankets you no longer like. Sell or donate them! Do you have 100 children's books constantly being thrown on the floor? Donate the ones which are no longer age appropriate or enjoyed by your children and only keep the special ones. Supplement with library books!

Can't find a way to display all your decor, but you've edited as much as you wish to? Rotate it! Keep a small box of stored decor and swap it out every now and then for a fresh look rather than buying new.

Edit, edit, edit. And then reconsider your haven mission statement and brainstorm storage or organizational solutions to help a small space work for you.

8. You're A Haven Maker

Congratulations! You're officially a haven maker. You've chosen to arm yourself with the tools necessary to transform your house into a haven. You've taken the steps to design a life inside your home. You've joined the club of haven makers.

I'm so grateful to be able to help walk you through this process as you seek to improve the home you have and love where you live. Continue to evaluate this 10 step process with each project you tackle to keep your home cohesive and keep your mindset aligned.

And don't forget to enjoy the journey! Let the 10 step process take the stress out of home updates and take it one day at a time. You've got this.

For daily inspiration and ideas, visit my blog www.graceinmyspace.com and join me on my own journey of creating a haven.

Leave a Review

I'd love to hear from you! Please leave me a review on Amazon on your thoughts on this book and corresponding workbook to share how it has helped you or how I can improve! I value your feedback immensely.

WORKBOOK

Designing a Life: From House to Haven

Fill a house with decor and it remains just a house. Design a life-giving space and it becomes a haven.

Now that you've learned different strategies and techniques to approach designing your home to be a haven, you can use this workbook to walk through the basic steps in the design process.

Whether you are renovating an entire home or just freshening up one room, use this method for **every new project** you want to accomplish.

~Sarah
www.graceinmyspace.com

Step 1: Know Yourself

Think about your personality. Write down 5 words that define you as a person. Next, write down 5 words that define the people who reside in your home with you. Use additional paper if necessary.

_____

_____

_____

_____

_____

_____

_____

_____

_____

Create Your Haven Mission Statement

Define Haven:

_____

_____

_____

_____

_____

_____

_____

_____

_____

_____

What is your desired Atmosphere?
_____

_____

_____

_____

_____

_____

_____

_____

Determine Life Goals:
_____

_____

_____

_____

_____

_____

_____

_____

_____

State Your Haven Mission Statement:

_____

_____

_____

_____

_____

_____

_____

_____

Step 2: Define Your Needs

What Makes You Tense?	What Makes You Relax?	Time Limitations	Space Needs

Define Your Needs: Write down as many needs as you can think of. This can be anything specific from room sizes, type of home (apartment v. ranch, etc.), number of bed and bathrooms, to color palettes that fit your personality.
Also, think about what your home will be used for. Ex: Business, family needs, entertainment...etc.

_____

_____

_____

_____

_____

_____

_____

_____

_____

Step 3: Evaluate the Problem
Define the elements in your home that are currently preventing you from enjoying a haven.

_____

_____

_____

_____

_____

_____

_____

_____

Write down the specific problem(s) you wish to solve.

_____

_____

_____

_____

_____

_____

_____

_____

_____

Specify the scale of your project. Circle all that apply, specific to each project.
Rearrange.
Refresh.
Remodel.
Renovate.

Step 4: Set Realistic Expectations
Use the space below to write down expectations for EACH PROJECT under each category.

Project:

_____

Budget:

_____

Limitations:

_____

_____

_____

_____

_____

_____

_____

_____

Timeframe:

_____

_____

_____

_____

_____

_____

_____

_____

_____

Your Ability v. Need for Contractor/Designer:

_____

_____

_____

_____

_____

_____

_____

_____

_____

Step 5: Create a Design Vision
Using Pinterest, create a separate board for every project you intend on completing. Fill each board with inspiration photos that pass the "stop and stare" test.

Step 6: Define What Makes Your Heart Sing
Study other people's design. Use your Pinterest boards, magazines, Instagram, blogs, or design books and write down the *specific elements* that draw you in.

_____

_____

_____

_____

_____

_____

_____

_____

_____

Step 7: Narrow Down Design Plans Based on Needs

Compare your list of needs, budget and limitations to your list of elements that make your heart sing. Cross off any design elements that don't fit your needs, budget or limitations.

Needs, Budget, Limitations

_____

_____

_____

_____

_____

_____

_____

_____

V.

Design Elements That Make Your Heart Sing

_____

_____

_____

_____

_____

_____

_____

_____

_____

_____

Below, write down the remaining elements that you believe you could realistically incorporate into your design plans.

_____

_____

_____

_____

_____

_____

_____

_____

_____

Step 8: Create Short Term + Long Term Goals
Keeping in mind your haven mission statement, needs, realistic expectations, and the narrowed down list in step 7, create 3-5 short term goals and 2-3 long term goals (depending on your project size). Be specific!

Short term goals should be able to be completed within a month.
Long term goals can take anywhere up to 6 months-1 year.

Short Term Goals:

_____

_____

_____

_____

_____

_____

_____

_____

Long Term Goals:

_____

_____

_____

Step 9: Edit Your Existing Decor
Use the space below to write down the main decor items in your home. Separate them by category. Love It. Repurpose It. List It.

Love It.

_____

_____

_____

_____

_____

_____

_____

_____

Repurpose It.

_____

_____

_____

_____

_____

_____

_____

_____

_____

List It.

_____

_____

_____

_____

_____

_____

_____

_____

_____

Step 10: Implement

Now that you've done all of the prep and pre-design it is time to implement! Write out your design plan below. Keep in mind your haven mission statement and let your short and long term goals guide your plan:

_____

_____

_____

_____

_____

_____

_____

_____

_____

_____

_____

_____

_____

_____

Printed in Great Britain
by Amazon